Original title:
Life: A Journey Full of What Ifs

Copyright © 2025 Creative Arts Management OÜ
All rights reserved.

Author: Thomas Sinclair
ISBN HARDBACK: 978-1-80566-145-0
ISBN PAPERBACK: 978-1-80566-440-6

Footsteps in the Fog

I took a step into the mist,
Wondering where I really missed.
A squirrel waved, then dashed away,
I guess it doesn't care to stay.

With each footfall, doubts arise,
Is this a path or just bad pies?
A shadow laughs, I hear it call,
Did I just trip? I'm bound to fall!

Navigating the Unknown

Maps are handy, or so they say,
But I just run and hope to play.
A signpost points to who-knows-where,
Should I go left or take the dare?

With every turn, a giggle grows,
I ask a duck which way it goes.
It quacks in joy, it seems to know,
I'll follow it, wherever it shows!

Moments that Could Have Been

I could have danced, but tripped instead,
And now I twirl in dreams instead.
A pizza slice that went untouched,
Should I have nibbled? I'm so crushed!

At parties where the funmen laugh,
I ponder deep, my heart's a calf.
Forgot my hat, what a surprise,
Now I'm just the hatless guy!

The Forks of Fate

Two paths ahead, what a delight,
One leads to heights, the other fright.
I take a breath and pick a side,
Did I choose well or just abide?

There's cake to my left and brussels sprout,
I ponder life, as crumbs fall out.
With forks like this, how could I know?
Next time, I'll just stick to the dough!

Twilight of Opportunities

When dawn's first light tickles your face,
And you ask yourself, 'Should I leave this place?'
You ponder each choice like a game of chance,
What if I jump? What if I dance?

With breakfast burnt, your toast in the air,
You wonder 'What if I just didn't care?'
The clock ticks louder, a comedic race,
Dashing to work in your mismatched lace.

You sit in a meeting, and doodle a cat,
Imagining fame from a viral chat.
But what if the cat gets more likes than you?
Then you ponder your dreams in a coffee brew.

As twilight descends, you reach for the night,
What if tomorrow I take to flight?
With stars as your guide and your heart in a whirl,
You giggle at what-ifs like a playful girl.

The Awakening of New Paths

The sun peeks over hills, a whimsical smile,
You wave at your choices from afar with style.
With pancakes flipped high like a chef on a spree,
'What if it's Tuesday? Should I sip my tea?'

A stroll through the park leads to bushes that sway,
What if the squirrels talk? They might have their say!
You mutter your dreams while pretending to jog,
While pondering recipes for a feisty frog.

The train whirs by with a curious squeal,
What if I hop on without any meal?
But buffet awaits, and you're full of delight,
With trips to the kitchen, an endless appetite.

As evening rolls in, the path feels so bright,
You wander and wonder, what's left in sight?
With laughter and charm, you dance like a wave,
In the unusual twists that your choices behave.

Paths Not Taken

A shoelace tripped me, oh what fun,
Did I choose the right path, or just run?
I could have been a chef, making stew,
But here I am, outside chasing a shoe.

The ice cream truck calls, but I must resist,
What if I were a juggler—oh, that's a twist!
With flaming batons and a cheeky grin,
But instead I'm here, trying not to spin.

Whispered Possibilities

In a world where cows wear polka dots,
What if I had danced with them in knots?
A llama in shades might join the spree,
But I'm stuck here sipping a cold cup of tea.

Imagine the squirrels, plotting and scheming,
While I'm just daydreaming, endlessly dreaming.
Would I be a king, or a prince with a cap?
Or perhaps I'd just nap on a giant map?

The Fork in the Road

At the fork in the road, I paused for a snack,
Should I head to the left or should I go back?
A chicken in sunglasses said, 'Stay awhile!'
So I plopped down and shared a silly smile.

What if I had taken a plunge in the lake?
Would I have come out as a fish or a cake?
The choices are endless, twirling around,
Still laughing at how I fell on the ground.

Unwritten Tomorrows

Oh, the tomorrows that tease and await,
One is a party, but I'm stuck at a gate.
What if I wrote the next great hit show?
Or decided to build a miniature dojo?

The clock keeps ticking, my plans go astray,
What if I just slept the entire day?
But here comes the mailman, with a grin on his face,
Shouting, 'Tomorrow's a party—come join the race!'

The Essence of Maybe

In a world of could-be's,
I wear mismatched shoes,
What if I choose tea?
Or a dance in the blues?

Perhaps I'll start a band,
With a cat as my lead,
Playing tunes on demand,
For folks in need of heed.

If wishes were horses,
I'd ride 'em to work,
But they'd trip on their forces,
And leave quite a quirk.

Yet here I stand, bemused,
With options aplenty to see,
In this game, I'm amused,
What's next? Who's to decree?

A Puzzle of Tomorrow's Hues

Pondering my breakfast,
Should it be toast or pie?
An omelette's a fine quest,
But wait—what if I fly?

Colors splash the canvas,
Of plans unmade, so bright,
What if I paint a cactus?
In shades of green and fright?

Pictures swirl, then fade,
As I step on a crack,
What if the price is paid,
For a whimsical snack?

Every choice, a riddle,
Woven with humor and cheer,
In the game of the middle,
Tomorrow's hue draws near.

Navigating the Unseen Currents

Drifting on thoughts adrift,
With a map drawn in jest,
What if I sail a gift,
On seas that never rest?

Waves of wishes around,
I paddle with a spoon,
What if I make a sound?
That charms an owl or moon?

Clouds gather with delight,
In a sky made of sass,
What if I catch a kite,
With jokes as my compass?

Through each twist and turn,
Of paths unseen, I roam,
The laughs that I discern,
Bring me back home.

The Haze of Potential

Fog rolls over my dreams,
Whispers? Or just my snacks?
What if all is as it seems,
Or maybe I need more snacks?

I trip on grand ideas,
Like slippers left behind,
What if I juggle fears,
And let the chaos unwind?

The fog thickens, I laugh,
As questions dance and swirl,
What if I take a path,
Made of chocolate and twirl?

Yet, in this misty maze,
Adventures I can't resist,
With humor that stays,
What's lost may still exist.

The Path of Shadows

As I stroll down paths unknown,
I trip on thoughts I've never sown.
Maybe crabs can play the flute,
Or kangaroos can wear a suit.

I ponder thoughts like silly games,
What if my dog could throw my frames?
And who decided that cats hate rain?
Perhaps they just enjoy the pain.

I chase my dreams on roller skates,
While dodging all those birthday plates.
With every laugh, I feel more spry,
But who knows why I always sigh?

If only fish could laugh and jest,
Or wear a tiny, dapper vest.
Yet here I am, just getting by,
Wishing I could learn to fly.

Echoes of Unexplored Moments

In shadows cast by gleeful times,
I wonder if my goldfish rhymes.
What if clouds were made of cheese?
I'd catch them all with joyful ease.

What if my shoes could dance for me?
To waltzes sung by bumblebees.
If only squirrels would share their nuts,
Instead, they take their little struts.

Imagine trips on flying pies,
Where dinner rolls and laughter rise.
I'd skip the mundane, leap and bound,
Through echoes lost, then joyfully found.

With each new twist upon this trail,
I'm ever curious, without fail.
What if the sun could wear a hat?
Or pigs could chat, and that was that?

The Journey Within the Journey

I set out on a curious quest,
With snacks and dreams, I'm truly blessed.
What if my map leads me astray?
To a land where ducks can dance and play?

Each step unveils a new delight,
Like chocolate rivers that glow at night.
What if every tree could sing?
Then I'd be crowned the dancing king!

As I wander, my mind flips,
What if I could wear potato chips?
With laughter echoing on the way,
I'll munch and crunch, come what may.

So here I twirl, a joyful sight,
In a world of giggles, dreams take flight.
With every turn, a joke to share,
I roam the path without a care.

Forks Beneath Falling Leaves

At forks in roads where colors clash,
I ponder life with giggles and a dash.
What if a leaf could fly and text?
It might say, "Pick me! I'm not vexed!"

I linger long, the choices swirl,
With playful thoughts in crazy twirl.
Could turtles slide on rainy streets?
Or wear tiny shoes for their little feats?

With every turn, my spirit sings,
What if I could hug the spring?
And plants could dance to funky beats,
While I just waddle with happy feets?

So down I skip, with laughter bright,
Through golden leaves and pure delight.
At each new fork, I'm quite inclined,
To see the funny side of mind.

Fables of Choices Unmade

In a land where choices frolic and play,
A squirrel debated, should he seize the day?
He chose a nut but tripped on a shoe,
Now it's a dance that the forest crew grew.

The rabbit pondered on what to wear,
Should it be purple? Should it be rare?
He donned a hat, but forgot the pants,
Now he prances, if it ain't romance!

Dreams on the Wind

A kite flew high, chasing dreams with zest,
It tangled in clouds, what a grand jest!
Each tug was a giggle, each swirl was a cheer,
But down came the kite, oh dear, oh dear!

A fish thought to swim with the birds above,
"I'll fly, it's a plan that I truly love!"
But flippers and feathers don't quite align,
So he swam in a pond, declaring, "I'm fine!"

What Paths May Whisper

Two paths were laid out, which one to choose?
One looked cheerful, the other, a ruse.
One had daisies, the other, a trap,
You guessed it, folks, he chose the wrong map!

A pair of shoes shouted, "Pick us, oh please!"
The other was silent, hidden with ease.
He danced his way home, left and then right,
Tripping on poodles, what a silly sight!

The Road Yet Taken

There's a road out there paved with marshmallow dreams,

It beckons with giggles and bright shiny beams.
But watch out for gumdrops that stick to your shoe,
They'll slow down your journey and turn you askew!

A traveler stood still, pondering which lane,
Should he take the left or the one filled with rain?
In the end, he skipped through a field of delight,
Hopping on jellybeans, what a curious sight!

Whispers of Regret

I chewed my nails on the bus,
Wondering what if I'd made a fuss?
Should I have danced on that café table?
Or just sat quietly, feeling unstable?

The cat I named Sir Fluff-a-lot,
Might have been a tiger, I forgot.
What if I'd been a circus clown?
Or decided to wear a shiny gown?

Each day spins a fresh fool's errand,
With whispers I hear from every strand.
What if I skipped lunch and ran?
Would I be a hero or just a fan?

But here I sit, with a pizza slice,
Pondering choices that weren't so nice.
What if I'd eaten all my greens?
Would I wear tights and have crazy dreams?

Riddles of the Heart

A heart in a blender, what a sight,
What if I confessed on a midnight flight?
Should I have written that love note and cried?
Or stuck to my plan of letting it slide?

I sent my heart to a hundred doors,
But only found my old socks on the floors.
What if I just dressed like a bold peacock?
Would that charm anyone, or just make them mock?

A dance at the mall could've changed my fate,
But I tripped and fell, oh, isn't that great?
What if I asked the barista to dance?
Instead, I just stood there, missing the chance?

Now I giggle at memories made,
Of awkward moments and plans delayed.
What if dancing's where love takes a start?
Could it be simpler than riddles of the heart?

Chasing Possible Selves

I tried to be a rock star last week,
But my voice sounded like a duck with a squeak.
What if I'd trained with a golden throat?
Would the world feel my musical note?

I could have been a serious chef,
Cooking pasta that made hearts feel left.
What if I flipped pancakes in the sky?
Would they bring laughter or merely a sigh?

Each day I chase a funky new me,
Like a squirrel juggling nuts from a tree.
What if I were an astronaut, oh so grand?
Flying through space with a taco in hand?

But alas, here I am, in my sweats,
Making crazy plans with no regrets.
What if I'm already who I should be?
Just a curious soul chasing what's free?

Strands of Destiny

With each strand of hair, a story unwinds,
What if I had chosen different kinds?
Should I have been a magician in France?
Or a poet who dreams, taking bold stances?

I once wore socks that didn't quite match,
What if I'd tried to create a new batch?
A trendsetter's cap or gigantic shoes?
Instead, I sit here, just trading my blues.

What if my future's a jigsaw of chance?
Each piece a decision—should I take a glance?
Waltzing with fate sounds grand and sublime,
But I trip on the sidewalk every old time.

Yet here I am, creating my fate,
With laughter and quirks, isn't it great?
What if the path is a path made of fun?
Then bring on the silliness, let's all run!

The Dance of Might and May

In the garden, daisies sway,
Might and May do laugh and play.
Maybe we'll find a lost shoe,
Or catch a frog that sings 'foobar' too.

What if squirrels wore tiny hats?
Would they tip them to us—perhaps?
While dancing on a tree branch high,
Their tightrope act makes the pigeons sigh.

A cat walks by with a puzzled stare,
Thinking, 'Did I just see a bear?'
Each step we take has room for more,
From twirls and spins to the front door.

So let's not worry, let's just laugh,
As might and may take a funny path.
With each misstep, we find our grace,
In this silly, whimsical chase.

If Only the Stars Aligned

If only the stars had better plans,
I'd be president, not in bands.
The moon would dance in polka dots,
While aliens play the tambourine like tots.

Comets would help us cook a meal,
With shooting stars that burst and squeal.
Yet here I stand with cereal toast,
Dreaming of beings I can't even boast.

Oh, the traffic jam up in the sky,
Where space cows laugh and planets sigh.
With each wish made in childish delight,
Who knew the cosmos could be so polite?

So let's raise our glasses—toast the absurd,
To stars misaligned and futures deferred.
In this magical dance of whimsical lore,
We'll giggle at dreams we strive for, and more.

Hidden Roads Awaiting

On paths where no one dared to tread,
I found a sign that quietly said:
'Welcome to wobbly, wonky town!'
Where ups are downs, and smiles won't frown.

The trees wore glasses, quite a sight,
Chasing shadows in the warm moonlight.
Roads twist like candy canes galore,
With zigzags leading to a marshmallow store.

I met a turtle who raced with glee,
While singing songs about spaghetti.
He winked and said, 'It's all a charade,
Life's just a game, oh what a parade!'

So let's wander down these quirky lanes,
Where ups and downs are all just gains.
With laughter echoing through the air,
Every hidden road has wonders to share.

Conversations with Time

I sat with Time on a picnic rug,
She spilled her tea, then gave a shrug.
'What if clocks could dance a jig?
Would that make us feel less big?'

'Oh, dear friend, what a thought!'
She chuckled, 'Maybe make time rot!'
As seconds tripped on my distraction,
I pondered absurdities with satisfaction.

Time whisked her hair like windswept leaves,
Said, 'Stop and smell the silly thieves.'
While I sipped coffee, black as night,
We sculpted dreams with sheer delight.

So let us wander, unafraid of change,
In this quirky game, oh how strange!
With Time as my partner, I shall defy,
To dance through moments, oh me, oh my!

The What-If Compass

What if I took the left at the light?
Would I find treasure or just a fight?
Maybe there's cake waiting just ahead,
Or a clown with balloons who'd rather be fed.

What if I danced instead of just stood?
Would I trip and fall, or make it look good?
Perhaps I'd invent a wild new dance craze,
And become a sensation in a hundred reviews!

What if I called a friend from the past?
Would they giggle or say, 'Wow, that's a blast!'
Or would they hang up, phone fading to red?
Just another 'what if' stuck in my head.

What if I flipped a coin for my fate?
Heads, I win! Tails, I can't relate!
Or should I just stay in and binge watch a show?
What if I'm destined to never quite know?

The Mirage of Yesterday

What if I could rewind to that very place?
Where I ate too much cake and got whipped cream on my face?
Would I laugh at the past, or feel a small frown?
Picturing myself in that silly old gown.

What if I saved every piece of advice?
Would I be wise or just thinking twice?
I asked once for wisdom, got fries instead,
Fast food reflections swirling in my head.

What if I skipped that day I wore stripes?
Would the world be the same without mismatched types?
Or maybe a fashion icon I'd be renowned,
For sporting the craziest looks all around.

What if the laughter could echo all night?
Would it fill up the air, making troubles take flight?
Or just a mirage, a fleeting delight,
Chasing shadows of joy in the thick of twilight?

Imprints of Imagined Roads

What if my shoes could walk different paths?
Would they bring me to laughter or stir up some wraths?
Maybe tripping on dreams left behind,
Discovering wonders I never could find.

What if my map had a riddle or two?
Instead of directions, just nonsense to woo?
I could solve for adventure or wander in vain,
Stuck in a puzzle driving me insane!

What if I planted a tree in a blink?
Would it grow apples, or just make me think?
Maybe it's a fountain of endless good cheer,
Sprouting wise words for all who draw near.

What if the road twisted, looped like a ride?
With ups and downs that we can't help but glide?
Navigating curves with smiles so bright,
What a wild trip that ends in delight!

Tides of Futurity

What if I sailed on tomorrow's great waves?
Could I surf on a whim, or would I be a knave?
Maybe I'd catch a glimpse of what's there in store,
Or find a sea monster who just wants to roar.

What if I shined bright like a beacon at sea?
Would the ships all steer clear, or think, 'Look at me!'
Casting nets of laughter across every star,
Instead of worrying how close or how far.

What if I danced with shadows of glee?
Twisting and turning, just feeling so free?
Would the moon grab my hand and twirl me around,
Or would I just stumble and tumble to ground?

What if tomorrow is wrapped in a grin?
Posing for pictures, capturing skin?
With moments so quirky, absurd as they seem,
We'd stitch together a wild, funny dream.

The Time That Slipped

I woke up late, missed my train,
A cat sat smug, without a chain.
What if I ran, what if I tripped?
Turns out the universe just whipped.

Coffee spilled on my favorite shirt,
As I rushed, I danced in the dirt.
What if I'd sipped, oh so slow?
I'd be on time, or not, who knows?

A bird flew by, gave me a stare,
What if I asked, 'Do you care?'
Instead, I slipped, fell on my face,
In this chaos, I found my place.

So here I stand, a little late,
With laughs and spills, I celebrate.
What if I change how I begin?
Maybe next time it's all pure win!

Crossroads in the Twilight

At a fork in the road, I scratched my head,
One path had cupcakes, the other dread.
What if I choose, the sweet delight?
But what if the cake was a terrible bite?

A signpost wobbled, gave me a grin,
"Take a chance!" it said, "Let the fun begin!"
What if I wander off and get lost?
Yet I'd rather risk it than count the cost.

The twilight danced, the stars said hi,
In the distance, a lone pizza pie.
What if I follow the cheesy scent?
Wherever I go, I'll be hell-bent!

So here I laugh, take each twist,
Every wrong turn is a chance I've missed.
What if I tumble, what if I soar?
Each crossroad's laughter asks for more!

Ripples in Still Waters

By the pond, I tossed a stone,
Watching ripples dance alone.
What if I throw a boulder large?
Would the ducks applaud my charge?

A fish jumped high, gave me a wink,
What if I dared to share a drink?
I fished for thoughts, come take a peek,
But all I caught was a rubber cheek.

Reflections laughed at my silly face,
What if I joined them in this race?
To skip the stones, to dream so wild,
I'd rather be a carefree child.

So here I sit, on the grassy shore,
Each ripple echoed, always wanting more.
What if this moment never shall fade?
In stillness, a million jokes are made!

The Paths We Veer

Two paths diverged, a silly fight,
One led to cookies, the other to fright.
What if I mix both maps in one?
A cookie monster sounds like fun!

On the first trail, I found a hat,
In the second, a very fat cat.
What if they teamed, what could they scheme?
A feline thief, or a pastry dream?

I tripped on laughter, slipped on a pun,
Chasing shadows, we danced till done.
What if I tumbled and got a laugh?
Every misstep makes a great photograph!

So I wander on, with silly cheer,
In every misshap I hold dear.
What if my mishaps lead to gold?
Each path I've veered has stories told!

The Allure of Almost

I had a chance to sing a tune,
But tripped and fell into my shoe.
The crowd erupted, oh such cheer,
For laughable chaos, I steer clear.

What if I cooked a gourmet feast?
Instead, I burned a toast to beast.
The smoke alarms began to wail,
My dinner party turned to jail.

Thought I'd be clever, catch a wave,
But belly-flopped, a different save.
Splashing around like a fish in air,
The ocean chuckled, beyond repair.

Dreamt once of scaling heights so grand,
Instead, I slipped on soft, dry sand.
The cactus showed me who was tough,
A twist of fate can be quite rough.

Moments That Flew Away

An ice cream cone, I took a bite,
It flew away, what a sad sight!
No one to share my creamy treat,
Just seagulls laughing, what a feat.

Caught a train, I thought, 'Oh, yes!'
But missed it by a second's guess.
Chasing after, tripped on air,
The station's crew just gasped and stared.

A chance to dance, my favorite song,
I spun too fast and twisted wrong.
The floorboard laughed as I flew by,
Another moment waved goodbye.

I tried to play the perfect card,
But ended up with something hard.
My poker face looked quite a mess,
But oh, the laughter, I confess!

Hushed Whispers along the Way

In quiet woods, I made a wish,
To find a catfish with a swish.
But all I found was slippery mud,
The fish just winked, then gave a shrug.

While walking paths I thought were neat,
I stumbled on a stranger's feet.
'Excuse me!' I almost cried out,
He chuckled loud, with joyful shout.

I heard the trees share secrets low,
But missed the point, a wild show.
The squirrels winked, 'It's just a game,'
As I pursued my moment's fame.

Along the road, a sign did say,
'Follow me for fun today!'
I thought it strange but gave a go,
Found nothing there, just high and low.

Constellations of a Dreamer

I wished upon a sparkling star,
But rolled over, there's my car!
Dreams of flight ended in snore,
My cat stared, and then, `No more!`

Map in hand, I took a hike,
But ended up beside a bike.
Thought I could ride, oh what a sight,
The wheels went left! I flew right!

Thought of sailing seas so vast,
But nearly capsized, what a blast!
The fish wore hats and danced a jig,
I laughed so hard, my boat went big!

In starry nights, my thoughts took flight,
Chasing dreams till morning light.
But sleep crept in, a sneaky thief,
Yet in that dream, I found relief.

Memoirs of a Maybe

I woke up this morning, should I have stayed?
Should I have worn shoes, or the flip-flops I played?
Should I eat toast or try pancakes instead?
So many decisions, I'm lost in my head.

Should I call my friend or just binge on a show?
Should I learn to dance, or just sit here and row?
With each little choice, I slip in the bliss,
But the what ifs come knocking, it's hard to resist.

Did I wear the right shirt or miss on the hue?
Do penguins wear bow ties, could I really ask you?
Each choice leads to laughter, or so they all say,
But I might just go napping, that seems okay.

So here's to the days, where 'maybe' reigns free,
With giggles and snickers as companions with me.
I'll wander this path, with snacks in my pack,
For in the land of what ifs, I won't look back.

The Heart's Diverging Trail

I strolled down the road with one shoe untied,
Decisions around me, I take them in stride.
Should I turn left or just wander the right?
I grin at confusion, it's all a delight.

I ponder love notes, sticky and sweet,
Should I write with a pen or with chocolate to eat?
What if I stick them where pigeons all roam?
Will they carry my message or head straight for home?

In this wild journey, what snacks should I bring?
Carrots seem healthy, but chips make me sing.
Each fork in the path, a giggle I share,
Oh, the wonders of wandering, with nary a care.

So here on this trail, I'll dance in the sun,
With choices around me, oh where to have fun?
For hearts like to wander, but giggles are free,
In the maze of choices, just let it be me.

Secrets of the Unseen Road

I'll follow my whims down this road of unknown,
With socks that are mismatched, in confidence grown.
Do I stop for some coffee, or tea in a cup?
The thought of my choices has me cracking up.

Each turn that I take leads to whimsy untold,
Should I swing like a monkey or stroll feeling bold?
What if I reach for a slice of delight?
Will it make my heart dance or lead me to flight?

I chuckle at shadows that follow my pace,
Wondering deeply, at what's their own place.
What if my laughter could echo and spread?
Could it tickle the universe right overhead?

So off on this journey, I'll laugh as I tread,
With questions and giggles that swirl in my head.
For the secrets I find on this winding parade,
Are what makes my heart sing, and keeps me unafraid.

The Odyssey of Choices

With a map full of squiggles, I start my grand quest,
Should I wear a cape, or just stick to my vest?
Decisions like clouds float, fluffy and free,
"Oh, what if I tumble?" says this silly me.

A fork in the path, oh dear, which way?
Do I follow the flowers, or the frogs that play?
Each leap that I take, leads to giggles anew,
What if the bumps start to dance with my shoe?

I'll ponder the colors of cakes far and wide,
Should I bake one with chocolate or stuff it with pride?
What if the sprinkles go flying on high?
Will the ants join my party, and wave me goodbye?

So here I shall play on this whimsical ride,
With choices and chuckles the heart can't abide.
From stepping on rainbows to splashing in streams,
Each path brings a smile, a dance in my dreams.

The Unwritten Pages of Time

In a world where socks always stray,
We ponder choices, come what may.
Should I take coffee or tea today?
What if I dance my cares away?

With each decision, a twist of fate,
Should I go early, or maybe late?
What if my cat just ran a date?
Or if that pie just sealed my fate?

The clock ticks on, and so we jest,
While certainly, we try our best.
If unicorns were here, we'd rest,
But now it's time for lunch, let's fest!

On pages blank, our giggles write,
The stories born from silly plight.
What if we dared to take a bite?
Of cake that glows in the moonlight?

Unforeseen Destinations

Off to the store, with a list in hand,
But end up lost in a rock band.
What if I dance with the nearest stand?
And win a prize that's totally grand?

Maps in our heads, we take a chance,
What if a squirrel joins the dance?
Wouldn't it be a fun romance
To see him twirl in tree-worn pants?

The paths we choose can be quite absurd,
Like picking a dog when you meant a bird.
What if I laugh and the world heard?
While munching snacks, that'd be unheard!

Through twists and turns, we spin and weave,
Finding joy in what we believe.
What if this moment's hard to retrieve?
Let's cherish our whims, we won't deceive!

The Flicker of Distant Stars

Distant lights flicker in the night,
What if they're watching our silly plight?
Stars giggle from lofty heights,
Their twinkles dance, oh what a sight!

Should one fall down, do we get our wish?
For pizza toppings, or maybe a fish?
What if they grant us a splendid dish,
With fries and ice cream, that'd be delish!

We dream of worlds, all bizarre and bright,
Where cats wear hats and dogs take flight.
What if we stumbled on sheer delight,
And turned our frowns completely alight?

As constellations align and play,
We ponder what on Earth to say.
What if each moment's a grand buffet,
Of laughter served in a unique way?

Stories Yet to Enfold

In the backyard, tales have begun,
Of a dragon that bakes, just for fun.
What if it's true, let's not be done,
With wild adventures just out in the sun?

Every corner hides a mystery,
Like a talking fridge—what a history!
What if it sings with such a glee,
And suggests snacks for you and me?

We scribble stories in the sand,
Of pirates who dance with a meringue band.
What if tomorrow brings a fresh strand,
Of whimsical wonders from a magic hand?

Unfolding pages, we giggle and share,
Making memories, light as air.
What if this moment's beyond compare?
With friends, a laugh, and zero care!

Hopes Wrapped in Uncertainty

Bouncing balls of dreams we throw,
In alleys marked by seeds we sow.
What if the cake's a mystery?
Or we find joy in history?

The chicken crossed, a bold delight,
To find a cornfield out of sight.
What if it met the other side?
In laughter, we take that ride.

The crickets play a silly tune,
While we all dance beneath the moon.
What if the stars could only yawn?
And sleepwalk till the break of dawn?

In a world of chance and dare,
We trip and fall without a care.
What if we wore mismatched socks?
And still, we'd raid the paradox?

A Map of Untraveled Ways

With a compass that spins around,
We wander where the laughs are found.
What if the road turns into stew?
And we dine on clouds with a view?

As we fold the maps with flair,
Discovering paths in the air.
What if a squirrel leads the way?
To frolic in the light of day?

Lost in thought, we take a pause,
Debating how to change our jaws.
What if the cheese become our muse?
And all we chew are happy blues?

We leapfrog through the fields of fate,
With giggles punctuating the wait.
What if we wore our shoes on wrong?
And danced to nature's silly song?

Reflections on the Edge of Choice

Standing at the fork in jest,
Deciding where to take a rest.
What if the pie ignites a war?
Or we find peace at the candy store?

A pickle jar holds time's embrace,
We try to catch a fleeting space.
What if our choice is a prank?
And we find treasure in a tank?

In the chaos, joy does bloom,
As choices dance within the room.
What if the socks start a trend?
And they become our greatest friend?

We spin like tops in dizzy fun,
Each choice a race, we've just begun.
What if we laugh till we just snore?
And wake to find we're lost for sure?

Facing the Unseen

Peeking through the curtains tight,
To spot the weird things start to bite.
What if that shadow's just a cat?
Wearing our fears like a silly hat?

A laugh escapes from behind a wall,
Maybe the ghost just wants to stall.
What if the unseen is just us?
Playing jokes on that old bus?

We tiptoe through the wobbly floor,
Imagining monsters by the door.
What if the ghosts just want a dance?
Or share with us their goofy glance?

So bring your heart and lift your chin,
Together we can face the din.
What if the unseen's just a grin?
A chuckle waiting to begin?

Uncharted Territories of Thought

What if the clouds were made of cheese,
And we rode them like a breeze?
Chasing dreams with ketchup fries,
Counting stars with silly sighs.

What if we danced on rainbow trails,
And wrote our tales in lemon sails?
With giggles booming through the night,
Imagining worlds, oh, what a sight!

What if the sun played hide-and-seek,
And we whispered secrets, cheek to cheek?
With every wink, the moon would spin,
Nutty adventures about to begin.

What if time wore mismatched shoes,
And we lost our way perusing views?
Laughter echoes from all around,
In this wacky world where fun is found.

A Quilt of Alternate Realities

What if cats ran for president,
With treats and naps as their consent?
Laws signed in purrs, they'd take a seat,
In a world where fish is considered neat.

What if toast could butter itself,
And cookies lived high upon the shelf?
In a pantry where desserts would charm,
It could save us from the morning harm.

What if socks could tell their tales,
Of long-lost shoes and laundry fails?
They'd form a band, a funky crew,
With mismatched rhythms and colors too.

What if the sun wore funky hats,
And danced with all the playtime spats?
With every laugh, we'd spin and twirl,
In this quilted realm, let joy unfurl.

Reflections in the Mist

What if mirrors showed our wildest dreams,
With upside-down smiles and chocolate streams?
We'd leap through frames, quite unrestrained,
In a world where nothing's quite as it seems.

What if whispers grew like towering trees,
And we climbed them up, swaying with ease?
Collecting thoughts in a swirling breeze,
Finding laughter buried 'neath the leaves.

What if hiccups sparked a dance-off show,
With funny moves and glowing disco?
Each giggle bouncing like popcorn pop,
In a misty realm where chuckles grow.

What if shadows tickled our feet,
And every step was an offbeat beat?
In this funny place, let's share a grin,
Where nonsense lives and laughter wins.

Palettes of Possibility

What if crayons could talk and play,
Painting stories in a bright ballet?
With every stroke, a new surprise,
Colors dancing before our eyes.

What if trees had hats of every kind,
And we could borrow, oh, how fun, how blind!
We'd wear them tall during summer's heat,
Mixing laughter with each silly feat.

What if dreams had flavors like ice cream,
And we could order the wildest theme?
A scoop of weird with a sprinkle of fun,
In this palette where all can run.

What if wishes were bubbles we'd blow,
Floating away in a playful show?
Chasing them down, what a delightful race,
In this colorful life, embrace the grace.

Turning Points

At every street, I stop and stare,
Decisions made with nary a care.
A left, a right, a spoon instead,
Did I just choose oatmeal over bread?

The callback call, I missed that day,
Napping in my park's bouquet.
A job I thought was oh-so-great,
But it was all just second-rate.

Should I have traveled far and wide,
Or settled in with cat as guide?
The answers dance like butterflies,
Or were they bees in clever disguise?

Oh what a ruckus, what a fuss,
To contemplate what's waiting for us.
With each choice made, a grin would stick,
Who knew that missing socks could click?

Tides of Might Have Been

The tide rolls in, it pulls and tugs,
What if I'd joined those cozy mugs?
A coffee shop or beachy bar,
Instead of pouting by the car?

What if I wore a swanky hat,
Or danced in shoes that were more flat?
Each wave of thought, each sandy toe,
Your guess, my friend, is as good as my show.

I might have been a world renown,
Instead, I'm just a goofy clown.
I'd trade my suit for flippers bright,
To dive in dreams each starry night.

The ocean's voice, it whispers low,
About the paths I'd never know.
But hey, I think I'll take a seat,
And let the roast and laughter meet.

Fragments of a Different Path

In the woods, I lost my way,
Should I have followed signs that say?
A map in hand, what more to seek?
But let's be honest, I'm quite the freak.

What fragments lie in every turn,
Do I embrace or simply spurn?
A skateboard here, a book left there,
Did I just miss the cosmic flare?

What if I'd chosen to sing instead,
In some Broadway show, not a sleepy bed?
Yet here I am in fluffy socks,
Trading banter for pile of rocks.

Each piece I find is slightly bent,
Like me in my old, creaky tent.
But laughter fills my heart so grand,
In this quirky, scattered land.

Navigating Maybe

Map in hand, I pause and squint,
Where does this trail of 'maybes' hint?
The local diner calls my name,
But will I win at this odd game?

Perhaps the sun will rise too keen,
While I debate if I should glean.
A taco truck or fancy feast,
I'll roll the dice, it's me, the beast.

Should I jump or merely wave?
Each second feels like a crooked pave.
With every smile, the unknown hums,
Making friends with unseen chums.

So here I stand, a curious bee,
Why pick one way, when all's a spree?
I'll zig and zag, embrace the thrill,
In a world that's silly, but oh-so-fill!

The Canvas of Choices

Brush strokes on a canvas bright,
Decisions made in morning's light.
What if I pick blue over green?
The masterpiece left yet unseen.

A splash of red, a dash of haste,
A painting made with all my waste.
What if I painted in polka dots?
My wall could burst with funny spots!

A tangle of colors, a patchwork scene,
Every choice, what could have been?
The journey's fun, with laughs galore,
Oh, what if I mixed shades I abhor?

In the end, I step back and see,
A quirky art, that's truly me.
With every stroke, a giggle sprung,
What if I painted when I was young?

What Lies Beneath the Surface

Beneath the waves, a sea of thought,
What if I swam with fish I caught?
A dolphin friend, a seaweed crown,
In this ocean, I'll never drown.

Octopuses dance, they twist and twirl,
What if they joined me in a whirl?
But then a crab offered me a shoe,
I laughed so hard, my dreams flew too.

Waves of options, flowing free,
What if I bounced like a bumblebee?
Life's a splash, a giggly ride,
Underwater, there's nothing to hide.

A treasure chest with silly goods,
Worms in hats, and fish in hoods.
So what if I never reach the shore?
I'll just swim and laugh some more!

Manuscript of the Unwritten

Pages blank, a tale untold,
What if I wrote of brave and bold?
A hero's plight, a villain's laugh,
A journey penned on my behalf.

Quills in hand, I scribble quick,
What if my plot turned into a trick?
A twist so funny, folks would cheer,
The chapter's end brings giggles near.

Characters tug at my sleeve,
What if I made them all believe?
A dragon who crochets in the night,
Stealing the show without a fight.

My manuscript, a silly quest,
With breadcrumb trails and a weird fest.
So what if my stories bring no fame?
Each page I turn feels like a game!

The Veil of Opportunity

A curtain drawn, a stage of chance,
What if I led a silly dance?
Jesters giggle, the crowd's delight,
With every step, I take flight.

Behind the veil, what do I see?
What if it's more than just me?
A parade of likes, and dislikes too,
Opportunities dressed as a zoo!

As I peek through, I'll take a chance,
What if I lead the grand romance?
With penguins waltzing, and cats on strings,
In this world, laughter sings.

So I'll lift the veil, embrace the show,
What if my bloopers steal the glow?
In the scene of chance, let's have a ball,
Dress it up, no fear at all!

Tracks in the Sand

Walking on the beach alone,
My footprints dance, then turn to stone.
What if I just stepped aside?
To chase a crab and join the tide?

A seagull laughs and swoops down low,
My hat flies off, what a show!
What if I let the waves take me?
I'd ride the whirlpool like a spree!

I play tag with the salty breeze,
But what if I trip? Oh, that would tease!
Each step a giggle, a slip, a grin,
Embracing the chaos, let the fun begin!

As the sun dips low, a golden hue,
I ponder paths that could be true.
But for today, I'll dance and prance,
In this sandy life, I'll take my chance.

The Echoing Question

In my mind, a question swirls,
What if I took more glittered twirls?
Should I wear a hat made of cheese?
And take on the world with utter ease?

I ponder if I'll ever know,
What would happen if I yelled 'hello'?
To cats, to dogs, or to a tree,
That just might start some great debris!

Each 'what if' opens a new door,
Maybe to dance on a dinosaur's floor!
Shout it out, or keep it tight?
Tomorrow's whispers will bring the light!

So here's a toast to silly dreams,
To wobbly thoughts and wiggly schemes!
I'll ask a hundred times with glee,
In echoes of laughter, I'll be free!

Fragments of the Unsaid

Left some words hidden like lost socks,
What if I told them, it rocks and shocks?
The thoughts tumble like a jumbled mess,
Could they be laughter or sheer distress?

What if I eat dessert for breakfast?
Oh, the fury! The sugary zest!
I'll write a note to my old toaster,
"Dear friend, you're a splendid roaster!"

In the jumble of all I could share,
Should I confess to my cat, laid bare?
That maybe I'm scared of the darkening sky,
Or is that just how the jokes go by?

Each fragment of thought, a balloon on a strand,
Floating above, reaching for land.
So here's to the whispers that tickle my mind,
Let the snippets dance free, shiny and kind!

Starlit Dreams and Dilemmas

Under stars that wink and twirl,
What if I swirled like a ballerina girl?
Would the cosmos giggle, turning round?
Or drop some moonbeams on the ground?

Each twinkle tapping on my skin,
What if I let the wild night in?
To ride comets in a silly race,
With space squirrels and a giggling face!

As I ponder my celestial plight,
Should I climb the clouds or just take flight?
What if I asked a star to dance?
Would it wink back, give me a chance?

Here's to the dilemmas that tickle my soul,
Will I find my rhythm, achieve my goal?
For in this starlit dream so vast,
I'll laugh at the whims, and hold them fast!

Between Dreams and Decisions

In the land of missed turns, we trot,
Deciding if what's missing will hit the spot.
Should I wear pants? Or go with a dress?
Oh, what a gamble, oh, what a mess!

With choices aplenty, I spin in my chair,
Should I bake cookies or just grab a pear?
The cake might seduce, but boy, it's a chore,
If only my choices came with a score!

How do we choose the right path to take?
With snacks in the mix, there's so much at stake!
Each tiny decision's like spinning a wheel,
Will I bask in success or will I just squeal?

In the game of what-ifs, I play with glee,
Trading my troubles for cups of iced tea.
With humor as fuel, I navigate haze,
Each laugh turns my worries into a maze.

Echoes of Alternatives

In a world of 'maybes', I sip my tea,
Did I choose the right sandwich, or just let it be?
Mustard or mayo, it's all such a quest,
As if on a treasure map, I'm searching with zest!

Should I dance like no one's watching, so free?
Or should I just stay and binge-watch TV?
Every single option feels like a hoot,
What if I wear socks just to shake up the boot?

I ponder my choices with a chuckle and sigh,
What if I fly, or what if I cry?
The paths we can wander are endless and bright,
But first, let's decide on a snack for tonight!

In echoes of choices, I spin round and round,
Wondering what's lost in choices I've found.
As laughter sets sail on my thoughts like a kite,
I embrace all the quirks, it feels just so right!

The Unknown Horizon

On the brink of the day, with my coffee in hand,
I dream of the places where I could stand.
What's on the horizon? A fortune or jest?
Should I trip over clouds, or just look for rest?

The map's upside down, or is it just me?
I'm stuck in a loop at a place called Glee.
With pointy decisions and marshmallow skies,
I laugh at the thought of my wild alibis.

Should I chase a rainbow, or opt for a nap?
With pancakes in mind, I'll take a mishap.
The sun might be laughing, the stars might just guess,
But wait, I forgot, I'm still in a dress!

At the edge of tomorrow, I'll leap without fear,
With a giggle and wink, I'm ready, my dear.
Adventure awaits in this whimsical dance,
It's all just a game, so let's take a chance!

Steps in Shadows

In the dimmest of corners, I ponder my fate,
Should I join the parade, or just sit and wait?
With shadows a-dancing, I'm looking for clues,
In the silly old game of the 'What Should I Choose?'

Do I walk like a penguin or strut like a cat?
Maybe I'll try something silly like that!
With giggles and whispers, the night takes a turn,
What's so funny here? It's just what I yearn!

In the steps of my doubts, I trip and I sway,
What if I break dance? Let's plan out the play!
Laughter's my armor, I'll wear it with pride,
In the humorous game where my choices reside.

So here in the shadows, we twirl and we spin,
With what-ifs and chuckles, let the fun begin!
Whatever the question, the answer's a grin,
In this journey of laughter, it's where we all win!

Resounding Footfalls of a Wish

In the land of might-have-beens,
I tripped on what I could have seen.
Each step I take, a twist of fate,
My shoes are laced with laughs, not hate.

Should I have danced or just sat still?
I took a leap, then fell down hill.
What if I wore that goofy hat?
Oh, life is funny, imagine that!

I had a plan, so grand, so neat,
Then lost it all in a snack shop treat.
Should I have ordered fries with cheese?
I grin and chuckle, oh, life's a tease!

So here's to trips with questions vast,
With every step, uncertain paths cast.
What if I fly, or what if I flop?
I laugh it off, I'll never stop!

In the Realm of Perhaps

Beneath a sky of cloudy thought,
I wonder 'bout the plans I sought.
What if I jumped, or danced on air?
Caught in the moment, nothing to spare.

In a realm where wishes play,
I ponder every silly sway.
What's this choice? Both pies look great!
I take a slice, then hesitate.

Chasing dreams like butterflies,
Some land softly, others fly.
What if I packed my bag right now?
Would I be lost, or friends somehow?

Yet through the laughs and strange might-have,
I share my tales, my silly salve.
In this quirky world of perhaps,
I find my joy in laughter's laps!

A Chorus of Could-Haves

In a symphony of chuckles and cheer,
I ponder back what brought me here.
What if I'd sung, or danced in place?
Would I still be sporting this silly face?

Each could-have bounces on my mind,
A melody sweet, yet unrefined.
Should I have waved or just stood stout?
The band plays on, I laugh and shout!

Imagining roads I never took,
Like that time I read a whole book.
Should I have skated, or stayed on land?
Hey, here's a giggle—life was unplanned!

So join the tune of whims and sighs,
A playful dance under bright blue skies.
With every could-have, a story's spun,
In this grand show, we laugh and run!

The Sway of Uncertainty

Twisting paths with each unsure turn,
I ponder all the things I yearn.
What if I'd tried to ride that bike?
But instead, I slipped—yikes! What a hike!

With socks that don't quite match my shoes,
I contemplate this path I choose.
Should I have gone for a fancy meal?
Or just dined on feeling surreal?

Every choice a wobbly dance,
Should I have flirted, or left to chance?
What if that joke had better flow?
I laugh it off, just watch me glow!

So here I sway with funny doubt,
In this quirky life, I dance about.
With every twist, a jest is born,
Embracing joy before the morn!

The What-If Mosaic

If I chose to dance on a sheep,
Would it bleat or just fall asleep?
What if I wore my shoes on my hands?
Would I trip on my thoughts, make strange plans?

What if the sun decided to rain?
Would umbrellas sprout from the ground like grain?
If I turned my socks inside out,
Would it solve all my troubles, without a doubt?

What if we swapped our morning brew,
For a potion that turned us into the zoo?
Climbing trees without any fear,
While squirrels take selfies, oh dear, oh dear!

What if the moon had a taste for cheese?
And all our wishes were made with ease?
With each little giggle, each twist and turn,
We stitch together dreams, for which we yearn.

Journeys Unimagined

What if we sailed on a cereal bowl?
With marshmallow islands, oh, what a goal!
Paddling past toasty flakes so bright,
Wishing on stars that sprinkles ignite!

What if shoes had a mind of their own?
Would they dance off to places unknown?
Skipping down paths, or stuck in the mud,
Creating a moment, a colorful flood!

What if we rode on the backs of our pets?
Through candy-floss clouds and silliness sets?
A dog with a top hat, a cat with a grin,
Racing through wonders, let the fun begin!

What if laughter could take us all places,
In silly old hats and comical spaces?
Building up castles made only of cheer,
Forgetting our worries, no stress ever near!

The Cloud of Uncertainty

What if the clouds had a taste for pies?
And raining is just dessert in disguise?
Baking up dreams in the sky so wide,
While we catch cherry plops with glee in our stride!

What if today I wore polka-dots?
And danced through the puddles, took silly shots?
Jumpsuits of colors, mismatched each day,
Inventing new trends in our playful ballet!

What if our fears came as tiny pets,
With their own little leashes and pasta-shaped sets?
We'd tour the unknown, have giggles and fuss,
In a world made of whimsy, just waiting for us!

What if the future was just like a game?
With buttons and levels, all dressed up in fame?
Unlocking the mystery of what lies ahead,
With laughter our compass, we'll boldly be led!

Letters to Possibility

Dear What-If, do you dance on the breeze?
With peculiar whispers that tickle the trees?
I wonder if wishes could ride on a kite,
Spreading their magic, oh what a sight!

Dear Maybe, what secrets do you hold?
A treasure map, or stories untold?
Would you take me to places I've never been?
In a land of giggles, where joy wears a grin!

Dear Perhaps, could we hop on a train?
With a ticket to fun, we'd never be plain!
Chasing the sunsets, giggling in queues,
With candy for supper and polka dot shoes!

Dear Adventure, let's plot a bright chart,
With twists and turns that dance in the heart!
Each what-if letter, a chapter to write,
In a whimsical tale that shines oh so bright!

Echoes of Tomorrow

What if I chased that ice cream truck?
Would I find adventure or just bad luck?
In dreams, I sprint like a gazelle,
Yet here I trip on my own shoelace as well.

What if I spoke my heart out loud?
Would friends retreat or laugh so proud?
A thought to ponder beneath the sun,
Maybe it's safer to quietly run.

What if I painted the sky so blue?
Or danced like a chicken in front of you?
The echoes call with a cheeky grin,
It's hard to know just where to begin.

What if I wore two different shoes?
Would they judge me or share my blues?
In the end, it's the quirks that stay,
And make this chase a flamboyant ballet.

Dances in Uncertainty

What if I wore my socks inside out?
Would the kitchen dance or just pout?
In this jig of bewildering spins,
I laugh at the chaos that often begins.

What if I asked a fish for advice?
"Go swim upstream," it says with a slice.
But here I am, stranded on shore,
Trying to tango with a closed door.

What if raindrops turned to confetti?
Would I dance in puddles, feeling all jetty?
With each silly hop and clumsy glide,
The world spins 'round on this tongue-tied ride.

What if my thoughts all had a parade?
Would I join the fun or feel afraid?
The uncertainty waltzes within my mind,
Yet in the chaos, pure joy I find.

Dreams on Winding Trails

What if I found a treasure map?
Would I dig in the yard and disturb the nap?
My dreams take me down a winding road,
Where squirrels are pirates and laughter's the code.

What if my cat would sing a tune?
Would the neighbors join or call it a boon?
Along the trail of whimsical schemes,
I chase after the giggles, lost in my dreams.

What if clouds turned into cotton candy?
Would I feast on fluff, feeling quite dandy?
As stars peek through with a playful wink,
I ponder the mysteries, giggling I think.

What if each step sparked a new song?
Would I skip to the beat, dancing along?
The trails may twist, but my heart knows the rhyme,
With dreams in my pocket, I'm never out of time.

Shadows of Choices Past

What if I chose to wear polka dots?
Would the world clap or throw me knots?
The shadows giggle from decisions made,
In the wardrobe of life, a funky parade.

What if I talked to mirrors that speak?
Would they offer wisdom or just critique?
In laughter's embrace on this wobbly floor,
The shadows remind me of what came before.

What if my lunch had a mind of its own?
Would the sandwich start moaning and groan?
With quirks of the past shaping my plate,
I nibble through memories, oh what a fate!

What if choices were just a big game?
Would I collect tokens or feel just the same?
In the dance of the past, I trip and I sway,
With shadows as friends, I'll find my own way.

www.ingramcontent.com/pod-product-compliance
Lightning Source LLC
Chambersburg PA
CBHW071834160426
43209CB00003B/297